Love,
Life Lessons

Erica Rayvon Hines

authorHOUSE®

AuthorHouse™
1663 Liberty Drive
Bloomington, IN 47403
www.authorhouse.com
Phone: 1 (800) 839-8640

Published by AuthorHouse 07/23/2019

ISBN: 978-1-7283-2046-5 (sc)
ISBN: 978-1-7283-2044-1 (hc)
ISBN: 978-1-7283-2045-8 (e)

Library of Congress Control Number: 2019910342

Contents

I am strong

I'm stronger than I ever imagine, I'm stronger than strong, a word of strength in my own bone... mental strong to physical strong I'm better than stripes, I'm pass of weak but path of strength, of our mind, I translate to ones being of ones hurt, Relations hurt on to others but that's not ones trait, a trait that's yours, a trait of mines, a trait of creations that I not but stronger than any pack, I'm of fine life on creations that's there to be, see, there to touch and cherish of destruction I made.. I'm weak of selfish needs of wanting to be hold, honored of beauty n knowledge, together I am strong but on my own of decite I am weak, perfect feet capable... I am able. I'm strong without the need of acceptance and one's soul... I can bare the rain, I can do the storm but one's spirit gets alone on reasons I'm made

Look

When I look into one's heart, I see life of ones not knowing about. ones not there, in the hole of one's deep, on music of no wisdom of acknowledge that wants to be sane, same, hurt and unknowing of other one, mind me, in need to be in you. what's best for us, for our well we are being good will future goods, bright and shiny of gold of diamonds bad of hurt n selfish of one's eyes I see along the decisions... one's heart empty only known of money. money make u happy or Love shall? What makes u me? What makes u feel you, what makes you, You? Life or Paper? Chains or Freedom? I see more than you... I see more than you Are. awesome without a dime... awesome without a leech, awesome you are, awesome without a hand

Clouds

Snores of yours wakes night bugs, in night crawlers of creepy things in night I take my fight in seek the night when light not moonlight nor sun is light, eyes hurt when I'm looking bright, at the light, why the sun hurt when I'm looking towards light? Why fire light in my eyes light? aren't the sun fire of light so why burn when out? Where clouds come from, where clear blue skies if royalty blue is light but clouds are not right? Earth outer beauty is not, on one a thousand years before light is light of experiments Killing our life, lives not woke, trusting in him, trusting in ghosts, trusting in souls that's gone, not ones that's easy to find

Comfortable

Waking up in the middle of the day, not searching of arms and breath is the
start of my day every week of every morning till day is night, I want to end
with a moment of all... of you, every touch is kind, & every look is fine, u make
my days short with seconds of sunshine, future thoughts I'm thinking when
doubts not there nor past weeks we shared, life is long, on external affairs
We share, shared, Neva taken or asked, agreements of yes and
no's we made, a relationship of love, sex, professions of confessions,
we're comfortable in each other sessions of progressing...

Shoes

Shoes, shoes, shoes, different shapes and colors, styles of generations, styles that die, styles that come alive, similar, identical, differences on 2face reasons, 2face heels on high heels and high boots, never shown on simple ways but high ways on request, demanded by popular faces on popular demand... we love we love, shoes shoes why must 40 pair? 2feet, 10 toes more cells, more toes, made on sole and core wouldn't be stepped...but stomped! Crafted & designed not a centuries work... one brain 2 shoes, 2hands, one mouth, 2ears, one nose, 2 smells... trust my heart because my brain is two, corrupted like 2 size shoes, trust thyself, love thyself, shoes are life

New

Islands of water, of sea water water of sea ocean waves of rocks of mold made of sea living ocean shells of sea creatures home taken from home to see more of what's there's in ours built on blocks in walls to keep home, islands I enjoy of great fruit, the sweet island the sweet taste of real islands, friends of friendly Islanders welcome here to welcome us the love to see n meet islands.. tress green green, must not taken from island that make island. Island sun, heat, teethe from more bringing n more islands around sea

Set

Goals, achievements, accomplishments, all little time to when stressed on many plans to maintain... one breath can skip the plan, Live in moments of care free life, Free choices an care Free mistakes is a carefree choice, life, ease the mind by less thoughts of things taken, of minds written for them for you on mine life, straight forward not coasters or circles of bumps n loops, life where choices n opportunities in many options available.. are apple friendly, healthy, saved and savored for your thirst of one's soul needed break from the hardened life they created, we created on mistakes n tricks for a better life. real benefits n life of easy acts in easy setting on BCE n DC way easy way when heaven was earth and life was right, overthinking and not thinking nor living will take hold, hold on good, hold on less, everything will rest, so just live in be set

Can't

Emotions on hormones of our ability of arousement of this cycle of shapes in positions of cries of sex and pleasant pleasing of pleasures you give, feelings I can't explain on given words in sentences a cry for you when whole inside of feelings I don't feel without you, deep in my vowels, I can't scream, speak, silent whispers I can't hang, silencence an faces of unbearable, unbelievable expressions I haven't seen.. a memorable feeling, I won't go without, a feeling only I have, a one u can give

Birth

Scared, lost, forgotten or empowered over is an emotion to come across through life, jobs, teachers and parents upon birth given unto, no needing to Feel hurt or Afraid while life of unknown possibilities in your wealth is waiting for you, courage to walk n run on the coldest of days, winter nights and hot mornings we wake, to weak, strong not resting of sleeping, we standing and breathing, I'm aware we living.. on my bad days, hard days of suicide thoughts of being strong I can't bear any longer, the fight on my behalf of threats n thoughts of abandonment n betrayal circles me in the middle of the night, that I can't hide from but giving up is not my way of deleting my wrongs, less caring n more doing on my behalf of happiness I am doing. To care for mine n to give me on mine is love, is a decision from you. the most high is you... doing what I want and accepted by you! is power, is love is courage, your love, your mind is courage from the day u arrived.

Good

Smoke from pain I conceived on past elations I once known unto ones heart I gave out unto many I thought I knew... dust in ashes on their behalf of my good Intentions... none I see or feel the past of many decisions I once made, haunted and abounded, never selfish I was, never spoken nor hidden, only hid from those I thought empowered me, scared to breath, scared to live, live the many things I'm made for, masks of images brung unto my good like clowns with shadows, shadow's once was light but destroyed unto missed confusions n voices once thought, once heard but interpt wrong based on images, sounds around you.. around us... made you and now live onto us... once I was there, the freedom calls inside of me, realization on I can't, live life on call ones and lost, & loses, the earth calls and I was steady and ready.

Sleep

Sleep where life is less and breathes are
Blind from life and blind from seen, care Free n careless, no moment, no setting,
just sleep not deep, not on death but death eternal, external, another life, another
of peace n kind... a joy of no thoughts n pain, no troubles but spirits surrounding
your sound of spirit of your spiritual life of your own world, of you, imaginations,
dreams on reality we make on sight, plots n forms of your peaceful being of what
you love when out, that pain of rest of you as they dwells in your favor.. to take the
right sight.. we fighting to make life bright... reality is life we make on choice on
our built, to be less of stress in shoulder looking but peace of naps, naps on stress, nap
press, drought, trough I can't rest... they make own life full when lids are right

Side

Love one in between another, of different sides of each other of one's soul connecting to be, ones soul near to be close... near more after, before to stay one, with mine with you we are one... in our shell in our spirit we hold on to faith, flurries of puffs, real puffs of our spoken word, spoken talent... to stay in move on from denials, demons, of bad choices on agendas of fail mentions, sin of things of made, created when self, belief we are one when together, when beaten, abuse and held back from pain, when nervous.. u is more than any being, anything from you isn't you, value of mind, soul, heart, of love of our joy of journeys that we see, our goals our future is planned here to be, to grab, take on life in the rounds of ages of us, till time, till life, till forever of our rounds for love

Know

Don't be offended on my way of good, speaking of bad and beauty... your mistaken for bad, mistaken for selfish, self-caring you are? Self-love is deeper than your way of doing, feeling, judging an seeing is only more manipulating than your Chicks n Self being, don't be hurt to truth, angered or foul, don't be bad for say I been here for your ages, more light than dark just hidden in the dark, where light is not notice, and worth is not known, only made wealth, only made love, hate they see while love they know, seeing your message on this Earth they hide from you.. don't be feared, envied is all they are, testing's of intelligence they joke on you, the difference they see in you, they need you

Control

Let's escape from the realities of mess, tired of
Annoying you, the lack that chills through spine...the winds you keep pushing through
time, our top covers n savors we never rewind, cuddles and fluffers fill the covers of silk
sheets in comfort of sheep. sheep we have, wear, sheep where are sheep? Counting sheep,
counting stars, without you what is sleep? Luclide, aware, beware the dreams we see,
reality just got so hard where the past decades are? Open presents, open gifts, open boxes
I'm so full of prizes, explore our options, explore our mind, take time, we have our mind

Choices

Motivation, motivation
I need motivation
To get me up n out
Healthy n bout
Bones strong like sprite
Up n I'm out
I need that for me, A need for man
I need motivation, to live on, move, to feel inspired
To be more than what's given, that lives threw us, our lives, every moment,
motivation is key, internal, external, internal rewards, honorable choices,
honorable people, honorable love. To be inspired, to be motivated. We all
live threw love n choices. I do what u do, be you, be me, you my strength my
inspiration, my beloved throttle, my hot mess, my disaster, I'm lovestruck for
you, I'm lovestruck for motivation. I live through me, you, us it's me.

Wait

I get tired of waiting
For you, for us, for commitment
You say this, you say that
I do this, I say that
Here we go, all again
Where we started, from scratch
A missing symbol there, a trademark here
Back in forth we go, around the eclipse we are
Again, and again, I try, I accept...
I Wait... You wait... We wait, For you. For us
For a life that strengths us, better's us and
Condemned us, for a life of happiness and evilness that stabs us all... That wakes us all
A side of rulers and lawyers, a side of quiet and shallow. A world of disciples of
discrimination. A life of roses and seeds all blooming to become more than just a mortal

Notice

I don't understand you
I barely like you
I love you
But moments I think,
I really think, Are you good for me?
Are you good for my health?
my heart? mind?
Days go by, months they turn
The lies resume, mixed messages
Mixed signals, Mixed judgements
Do you know me? Do you know me?
Everything I tell, do you listen?
Really listen when, Don't, Stop. Please... I'll leave
I'm a Joke?
Seriously.
I Wait for you, I wait for happiness. for us
Is love enough?
Is money enough?
Is my freewill worth it?
I don't know. I can't trust, I can't dream, faith, of actions an movement
Not Lip, misfortune
I'll get worse as days go, waiting, mopping, lifeless, you sucked it out, you
sucked me dry, when I offered help, self, when I offered you me, u take
advantage, served last, never first, never wealth. Today, tomorrow not lies,
not next not years. You see me you see face, unhappiness. Waiting for you.
Eating myself, shooting up, smoke in my mine, ashes of soul draining, listening
of voices drains me, my soul, my well, so I ask, are you good for me?

"I'm a Screw UP"

Bisexual, Homosexual, Straight
I'm me without my sexuality, I'm me w/o a Friend or an Enemy
I'm me w/o Someone judging me to be me, to fit in a world of deceit in betrayal
when Happy nor Sad, I'm me without you or an Upper hand
No one Knows, no one understands, why I do this? Or Why that? I'm me w/o
any approval or doubt, months to years... Decades even, you will not know nor Judge
You will not assume or erupt my doings, you Don't understand, u Don't Question
You don't ask. Just assumptions... you know it all... No Not
ME, Different an ways I don't understand, You or Others,
Doctors with PHD's And CNAs Don't even figure
I'm High n I'm Low I'm Happy as is, but Misunderstood Like a demon
I'm a Woman of Color of Good Deeds n Acceptance in understandings
n Unpredictability, A World full of Judges, manipulators and frauds,
I Won't Change..., I Won't hide! Why Change to be, why won't to be?
Picked on for thinking, knowing Acts of Mislead... but NO Not me...
U Misunderstood, I'm Ordinary in sane, Age With missing temps of
tags, I age, Growing to Create with People in my mind creating Should
of and Would Of's. I'm Not a Screw up for u not understanding,
I'm Not a fuck up for not seeing Different views in me may fittin n a world I Quite
don't get! Get me, I don't.... Depress runs threw me like a lonely Thanksgivings,
Christmas Eves...I fight... I Must Understand... I'm here... but NO

Accept me

No matter who you are, or what represents you, you're the image of you, no acceptance needed, no approval necessary due to the changes of you... that's all I want from you, not you for me, why change if love? If yours u accept me? Make sense right wrongs that's never a right an a wrong, no betters in no spirit, only a side tray, side piece, you'll never be whole without a entree, not self, not you, so why change you? Accept me

Question This

Real is power the fake is questioned, fake food is the taste of a real apple to a fake one, the sweetness of no bitter, tart or sour taste of real blessings from a false one, storytelling of false future's, of pain and depress, the sweetness of happiness and life all the answers you have to help life.. grow, live the sweetness of an apple, the answer is all answers, the difference between a scam and real is the taste of an Angel and a demon, care and careless, a real apple and a corrupted one, the dirt in the start of a flower is soul the start, to attack the inside is soul so ones soul is rotten..

Losses

Losses we go through at unexpected times are bearing to our souls once known and always loved, never forgotten, memories always taken, saved, shared, feelings of laughter, smiles we made, the bad and good, days is always a chapter of you, of us, better places than here... I wish I was with you, heaven and hell losses, we saved ourselves from me, how strong is mental, how strong is physical I can't handle the pain without you... keep me here, keep me safe, keep him away, know myself, know yourself you're in a better place

Feelings

Happiness within comes from self and love, stability and comfort, comfortable
with living and life on soul and life of many we help to live on, happiness is
a feeling not feeling but natural being one of perfection relieving of let goes of
created feelings. happy happy, we dance of actions to show happy, laugh, sing,
we must inspire within happiness to reveal true happiness, all self-love, of human
help, created help, damages created we see help without pride, grudges.
we need help to live, to fill complete! Help, if not, why not one? Show it! Show
feelings, show peace, show why we are, show how we feel, never hide the emotions of you

Love is Sacrifice

I Get lost... I forget all those Times I Went to sleep Lonely, Frustrated,
Exhausted, I Get to Wrapped up in your smirks and smart comments, your know
it all attitude, Your dirty Laundry... I get Lost. I Get lost in your politics
and your smooth talking, to get me to do something, to disagree but consider for the
hell of it, For the Love of it, for you I will, for you ill jump through quick sand,
obstacles and get lost in the maze, For you maybe. For me Yes, for Us Of course...
two Humans trying make it, two couples trying get lost in pleasure and pain
Cloudy Skies and Muddy Tires
I'm here through storms in sunshine
Through better or worse
My vowels remain true to two

Mine

Your craziness excites me in every way
U taunt and Scare and I stare and look
There's more to you than you think...
Your tough guy image.
It's just a front, it's just a shell of you
I see your soul, spirit... Your bad & your Good
You Can't get away from me
& I Can't run from you
You Mine & I'm yours. Our Craziness for Love and
Strength will Move us Further than night
No one can see but us, no one can bear but us
That fire and darkness, that light and sunshine... our
Tranquility and Love for one another... Is Stronger
Pieces

Stop! I Say
Your name haunts me in my shadows
It tears me open and Burns my Skin until bruised
I'm a Queen and a King, I'm more than one human
I'm more than one soul
I'm here & there
I'm everywhere
U can't be here & distant
I can't be rare and Noble
I can be brave & beautiful
Stronger n stronger I am

Recruit & fruitful
Only the real, only the Genuine
Only the smart & the willful
I'm better than I think
I'm better than you know
Confident I am & Determine I will
Doubtful I am,
My pride is Wrong, My Ego is me,
It makes me who I am, my spirit surrounds you, of good and bad of creations,
He surrounds me with love and hope he gives me joy and truth. I desire him more
n more I lust on my chest n between my highs love is here, lust is everywhere
Stronger n stronger I wont, like a tower I crave height of power
More of you I need, more of you I want
no more feeling weak...no more searching for answers I have...... All the missing pieces

Roots

Let's do it
One for the road
One round through solar belts, systems, of traction of tracks
the everlasting belt of planets of life roads
for the last being
One to connect our love an lust
We been down this road, to hell to heaven to hell to dirt to roots down
fire, down to the darkest of times to the saddest memories
To the happiest and joyous moments of life, memories to different times in
different scenes can be too much at times... Can be too much to others that see
us as crazy, likeable, weird, normal, no one gets and no one seems to hate... of
doing it, showing, listening, hearing of others is one road of feelings always told,
too much is never enough to for because someone to much is too overwhelming,
with happiness of your protection, with overwhelming care and attention,
we go down, down, this road with each other with confidence to conquer the hate and
the sea to conquer anything because we together as whole with Jesus our spirit

Deep

I hate you
I love you
My feelings cut deep for you
pass oceans, equators of large lands of life of inventions
Deeper than the equator
Deeper than there no words to sort
makes mad on full of hormones
U make more, more of us...
Love you more than anything else
Feelings depart onto your sin
Cutting u deeper than you imagine, cutting you deeper on good
Cutting u deeper than you never thought
Real love, true love, happy beginnings
That are endless,
Along as I'm here
I'll cut u deep into your success and fortune
I'll cut you deep into your actions and ego
Bigger than you, bigger than me
I'll cut you deep
Bigger than you'll ever know ♥

Gone

I want to be happy
I want to be near
I wanna live, live, live more than often
Cry less than children
Be happy n carefree, no worries, no fairytales just live life n joy
no rules, no commitment
No lies nor betrayal
Just happy n peace
No voices no temptation
No annoyance of broken things
No images of disrespectful and foul acts
Just peace n joy the Gods can enjoy
Just peace n joy only heaven can have

Don't think

I lay here in pain
Thoughts wandering, thinking hard of hard candy of bites drifting from life to death to Start to finish, stuck between letting go n being still, steady, Stable. hurt from lies n betrayal. Your love remains stable, my heart remains still. Wanting to love, wanting to care, not wants of evil n discreet but honest and holiness. Holy hell holy water, holy me holy ours, Auras in the air wishing over me, sun above me as clouds around me. I'm away, gone in mine, thinking of you n our...

Gift

A lifetime not enough
Time flies, like flies
Your words remain wise
A time to be remembered
A love to be cherished
Life moves us but we intervene
Between us, you n me
A time to love, to accept
A gift of understanding of us, easy life on happiness
A gift to us we give our hole
A spiritual gift we hold
Onto each other we obey
We loyal with a love that will never die
That will never forget, boast or brag
But to share a love like ours that exists
To our world that will never lie

More

So, the time has come
When I be me
Be free, be mellow, be me
Free is the power we all have
We all strive for to be, to sing, to fight,
To not have any chains or leeches
To speak when spoken to no freedom of speech, no peace, no word, no voice
No input or a say so, just commandments
& Demanding's, no please, no thank you
No External nor internal
Today was the day I posed to been free
From slavery, from cruelty, from wickiness to abuse. From
silence to voices, to happiness to tears, from high to low
Today was the day I pose to be free, once noticed I am free
Let go from lies, betrayal & commitment, shackles of lies of cages meant to go
Let go from you
The one I love, Care. Adore
One more chance, no more tries, no more we, us
One more chance
The faith I have, not you
The love I have not you
One more time I say...
No more times
I'm free

Must

I don't suppose to be sad right now
I don't suppose to be listening to other God's of Spirits created but ashamed of,
on well of other sins, dwells on my walk, my message, my way of building gods
future, putting me down, when high on life... to feel another's joy is perfect energy
when one is light, to feel another energy of selfish self is pain on my belief, my
soul, my whole of my spirit, my mind is my heart my heart is my guild,
...To stand n do more, stand strong and stand sleep, when not known because I Know
I'm going to be alright. I'm spiritual and can't be scar-ed, smears of less in smudges
of light, clear of night, made to be nice, to lift myself in any cant's, no less, no wrong, no
calls on missing ones cause we are strong when meant to be weak, I won't be sad in my
heart, I will care on my might, of myself n thyself, I won't be sad for others delight

Phones

Phones calls, and phone apps
Phone numbers n number problems
confusing like Lucy's lust, lost mind n lost heart, to make to destroy, to destroy is to
know, know how, and know why, to seek, why here n why now? Why apart, why near?
Confusing it is but confusing is hard & easy is life... To easy, too Right, just right
when no one hates on your light... phone calls is Wanting, wanting this, wanting that,
shouldn't be this, shouldn't be that.. gone on jackals, lifted by souls, Extra vests, extra bars,
fill me up with that center tequila on my created high... guys in joining cliques, cults,
squads partners, partnered by cuffs not whole... not one but scared of one... happy but lost
for say I am unknown not know of life not known of plans hidden in the unknown

See and Show

Who I'm I? As I look in the mirror in see a reflection of my mother and father as a whole. beautiful and mad, spoken as pain and light into the world of materialism of the world of hard work and worries... of beauty in the darkest of times to smile and play the game, to flick the lighter to ease my guilt... I carry beauty and wisdom in my direction to carry on a generation of lost and intelligence... stuck in the middle of night and day... I'm a whole of my being to spread talent of mine to another ones man... to be brighter than what is, to not tell but show the truth in moving minds, written words on spoken language that we created to be one with, other than family but enemies come n show there inner pain to let go in see the light of humanity... to let go in see you're not only. difference to be different, similarities to be whole. to not feel empty but carry on mine and yours in our new world that will destroy our humanity

Both

The greener the grass, the bigger the blessing, the receiving of our choices is brighter which makes us higher in the process of life in our forms of creations created. Of our Movements in transformation, of get together of families collide in our units of cubes, black and white on different set of views, tied down for a amount of time but brung together in light of thanks, thanks for a blessing thankful for a meal to share with you and me to the delight of laughter and nonsense, touches of light and sin collide in the most beautiful creation of earth downfall to fall up and down of nobody's perfect but see light in our imperfections.. to maintain in our home, we are bound to come

You

Man... life is so easier with you on my side, my thighs hold my knees
up and shoulders low as a relaxation of your love that takes the pain
down to deepest of the sea to fire of the light u bring by my side
.. your my heart, my life my peace that brings you peace to a peaceful mind
you have given me... our families, our love will bring them love, joy, hope to
find ones soul to come out n know there's Hope for everyone, to not give, u
gave happiness that money can't buy, that sight can't hide.. I love you and
your sight... to give inspiration you're the key to life... the key to love

Retail

We give thanks to our families, our jobs, our homes but more on to ourselves, to get
up each morning and rise to accomplish our goals, the stress, the pain, the laughter
we have in our times here, our times here Makin moves, sales and purchases,
to help to heal, to work together is to be one, a team we made and built on strive,
intelligence and acknowledge.. we fuss, we argue we disagree on opinions... but we
grow with another to get our spirits high, our spirits is here n watching, our mind is
up and racing but our work will prosper... our time here will always be remembered
to the beginning to the end, we would always be here, associates, friends, family..
our team here is bigger than retail, once left but forever in our memories

Unbelievable

Strength given to us, in a world of weaknesses n weak sins formed to make life easy on
weak unbelievable things we can't touch nor see told lies on earth weaknesses that we live
on but power of it we created n destroyed, the power within is the strength of our hearts
in the strength of our steps, the power of our mind is speaking with voice, letters that we
have power over, power on earth we have.. the strength of mind we abandon, used not for
good, acknowledge or presents bigger than gifts that we give of percentage and currency
but our minds n hearts are more stronger than things created, without this we wouldn't
be, without mind nothing is power, nothing matters when earth is dust... it's just rust

Who Likes Less?

Work is work no matter how hard or easy the position may be or how smart u might think, pay is more than a symbol, reward or cent, work is muscles moving between joints you haven't felt or seen, a motion of activity that requires your thought of physical n mental ability to move, make sense and make seen, appreciate of your work is known by manners I believe is a token of respect and treasure of good well and good being, of insides I do of kindness and need, the smallest gifts from the biggest minds, of potential I CAN's and I Will's, the smallest of the smallest gifts, I give on my wealth of selfishness I send of others I don't have, I won't have, work is my strength, spreading through my love on things I won't consider

Everyone Wins

Aspiring he is, aspiring he give me, aspiring he makes me when I'm low, not high on sin or good of being less, bad, more of what people love.. likes... not whole nor humans, spirits of start, the reason creations are here, in front of us I see more, deeper than now, deeper and easier no thoughts or thinking... but aspiring to know more, not creative or selfish or want it all but sharing Is caring... love is true, love is aspiring... love is found, easy sweet love... he I want to be, he I want to save, heal... how? Powerful of power hatred then made, evil was created... aspiring to be good, everyone loves, everyone wins

Be Beautiful

Creations we made to give us peace, home, comfort when we're not comfortable within ourselves, crafted and carved on evil agendas that jams doubts and insecurities in our mind, to buy to cherish on must haves the need to feel one within, within myself for; I have let Evil Win, Confidence need control over me shall I'll never brag once found.. perfect I am, I encourage others to live, be one don't win, don't spend on infections when your beautiful within, found or lost, it speaks when self, unfortunate, less or depress... more than life u is life, u are one who makes life and why we are... be beautiful, life is just a world made perfect

Know

Don't be offended on my ways of good, speaking of bad and beauty... your mistaken for bad, mistaken for selfish, self-caring you are? Self-love is deeper than your way of doing, feeling, judging an seeing is only more manipulating than your kick's n Self being, don't be hurt to truth, angered or foul, don't be bad for say I been here before your age, more light than dark just hidden in the dark, where light is not notice, and worth is not known, only made wealth, only made love, hate they see while love they no, seeing your message on this Earth they hide from you.. don't be feared, evilness it is, testing of intelligence they joke on you, the difference they see in you, they need you

Talent

Your talent and creations is you, that makes you perfect an a amazing way to know, to not know, to find, your beautiful of hidden talents u eager to find, u learn, you see what your mind can do, I'm happy I'm me, don't let people discourage you, haven't found, seeking, encourage more, be more, inspiration is love, inspirational is motivational, we must feel, we must know, leaders we are, made of love, made of perfection, don't leave me for finding my plan.. your power is your mental, personality is deeper than blacks of feelings high, your talent is your power, your power is Strength, personas you are, love your mind, love thyself, your talented n the most extraordinary way

Ayonna

Who to trust with precious souls out our womb...A gift from God, a Gift from the River that Comes from Our Garden, Our Seeds Grow into heads into little hands that reaches out for their life, that touches us every day through laughter and tears... To Chaos to Cheers of wonderful Steps in the mud to Bubbles in the Yard... Popping Dreams into Reality that we once dreamed of but Can't Live do to Anger and Abuse to the broken Souls of hatred and Deceit of Lies to the people we trust, to love and cherish to have helped but to hurt in the wickedness we live... To hold our Ones in the heavens we call earth to Live freely and pure of happiness and joy now turned into Bruises and broken hearts and bones to our ones waking up to... But not responding To wake up n not hear "Mama Mama" Let's play... Our Headaches turned into heartaches not once a breath taking away but Pride and Joy, we have that's crushed in dispute to loving relationships that once known...A prayer can heal, a Prayer Can Win, A Prayer can heal a thousand Wounds, but a Prayer can't heal that Voice that's already Gone... To push, to be remembered to accept and learn, to trust in him to love and Admire that She's better, a Heavenly Angel that Ayonna is, she is, an Angel That Speaks in plays and Praise over us to watch and Heal Her Families...

She Loves Us

Rip Ayonna

Heaven is Happiness-Erica Rayvon

Again

Disappointments are just a way to rethink and plan again, never give up nor rest up, set times and goals, go to remember disappointments are just a way to say it's not time, not ready or meant to be, not the time or place... go and find, hiding not here, hiding will never be found, win never sin, sadness is an emotion of care, don't stop the message to release is the message of death, disappointments come, we seen, we lived, don't give up we all learn, we all prosper

Family

Family, someone we should Trust, someone we should
care for, love n Be Given Chances...
Someone we Come together for... Our Morse Can't be done alone, to look
after n Shelter when n Pain... To Bring back to pieces again when in
Shame, your pain is my pain I Can't Blame or be Ashamed
We come together, but laughter holds us together... We Cry n fuse n do the most, we
steal we lie we human of spirits We Learn n Grow to Accept each other wounds n
success... we pass on each other traits and Do the same as one, u Talk I Talk We
are each other souls just passing by voices... Our lingo our walk our shapes and forms
through our hair lining to our finger tips I Can't deny a Sister nor Brother Art
thou Aunt to those who are Blood, no religious or partner should break us apart

Aroused

I touch myself when I think of you

Smooth skin Feeling me up through the thighs to my navel... Aroused when my juices perk up when you kiss one, one by one my skin tingles as my nipples perk out n soft, one touch 2 touch 3, I can't no longer wait to be touched by you... To my neck to my back each finger lowers me n holds me tight... I move I fight but I Can't... U tumble I fall u lift me up on top as I fill you up, fill me up when my eyes runs back n temptations take over. You mine now as you sweat n moan n my control, I feel you cumin but I hold, kissing you eagerly as u turn me on... I moan n arch as u kiss my back n grab my hair... I got where I won't you as my legs shake to hold on tight, I love it, I love it, our sex, firming and fighting gripping and sweating kisses like no other as I Ride you like no other deeper into Clarity, sensing your feelings your Touch... With me with you I Can't do much but make Kindness in our Bliss of lust and Temptations

Heartbreak

Smokes from spiritual ashes of fire burnt me, controlled me, you, past us on meanings of good life to fit the world ours, created you love us, what was us, we hide our truths, beliefs, our self of not knowing self. Knowledge on self not likes of self, self-worth, when, where, who I'm I? Covered in metal and tech of finer things hide us... we will never know us.

Commitment

A commitment bigger than life that's unplanned as plans... children, not planned but
given, not planned... a plan that's fast and unnoticed, choose us as one, ready, tamed,
ready to destroy, as bread, breed to heal to teach your committing to sin, your committing
to us, so fast, so soon, the natural being of love, the perfection I give, to teach, to heal..
your healing is bigger than the scare, you to kneel... kneel under the weak of pain,
weak of natural love, of you... you see who they see... now you see, committing to good,
committing to love, unconditional love, unconditional faith your good committing to good

Shadows

Guard me as you would guard knights over the gate, guard
your eyes, hide me in the light of your wings
Protect yourself from sin as he will take away your mind, Thoughts, Choices,
take care of yourself as if Jesus Lives within, (You) hide an take shelter
but don't hide in Walls, Share when needed, Share when Heard

Intellect Sex

Life more one, speaks, speaks of sex of life moves of move... centuries of sex, growing
of women intellect... two of Bringing love an sexual intellect I've seen without the
list of your sexual mindset... skin of fingers on mine touches light of natural feelings
giving's of yours onto mines, spirits of spiritual connections brings us our good in
bad, worst sides on betters of better... better with each other the sexual attention is less
than mentally attention the more of wants of intellect turns me on of mental trans
conduct of sexual tension you give, wet of intellect of touches of voice you sang to me,
preached of love and lust, Intel and less of shows.. a sexual intellect of mind over sex

Renew

A fresh start for the year of new beginnings, new places of creations of high that keeps us going, a fresh face to start a fresh Future, new dreams and goals that's there to be used, waiting in a world that calls for help a need for more of you, more of us one can't stand the lone of loneliness, a new line of loneliness never created of good of your mines of mine. Let's start new, let's start heaven on a circle of light and life

New Year

A new year, a new set, mindset, spiritual check, realty check, a new set of days of different hours different jobs of different meals, new tools new games new ways to manipulate the brain.. a set to excite the set you set to be you and not care of new but the same you, self and spiritual no man can come near he who self who there for he when he needs self (You) a new set of madness each year the beast to come never better but worse before past times was always better than now times, remember last time, last time was better, never good, not sitting not comfortable with now time within you, fight the new year, be the new year be better than you the earth will see

Friends

The friendship that makes ice with cream, charger to outlet, soup to bowl, water to soul, the friendship of life that grows more like we and plants grow, a friend that knows when wrong or my wrong n only true in right truths, relations that needed in need you bring me, brung me in my rights we gave each, u gave life, a voice of my voice witch made, a relationship is a you and me you represent me, the love of me the like of you, all of one you help me become me. You Saw me

Why I'm here?

Life moves on rather you ready or not, life is not a choice, life is not a game, we live and move to see more days, we didn't ask we don't know, why we here, what's my reason here? To find and succeed... not likely to fail when know how, new reasons to prevent from knowing, we grow on knowledge, lies to keep us going, don't tell what I want to know tell me what I need, life moves on rather right or wrong, seek answers and you'll be strong, wisdom is Key acknowledge is power, tell me how, tell me why, why I'm here? How I win?

I Know Bad

Woke up ugly daily of success, of self and love, I woke
up on a daily basis ugly on Others n Hate
I woke up in self-mind of others self-imagine, a mind of mine but a input of another's
recognize there ugly of imperfections. Of one's beauty by torture of insides are dirty and
Demolished of physical appearances of the sin of beauty, sin on others of sin on thyself
when wants over need of needs. Ugliness I am the beast of my appearance of another
one's statue of good, Evil, Destruction, manipulation and Corruption... I'm the inside
of ones outside... of mine inside of beauty, light, courage and intelligence shows from outside
in of blooms and rising, higher to highs of the most generous eyes on to myself... to stay in
be me, in my spirits mind, in my mind, to be the almighty right, that I can only be

Natural

Trust... Trust, I know what I'm saying but trust is not a feeling, trust is known, when u know well n know things that's given to you, born to, no question no reason to listen but hear too, ion want to feel, I wanna know, feelings that's deeper than words that's deeper than any feeling than any given human or.. a creation that started me, a feeling I don't know what's coming but my being is the start, the surroundings revealing, when I'm up in grooming, blooming, in today's economy of many loses of one's soul been forgotten.. not living nor breathing but choking, separated from life departed from heaven unto morality, being honest to love is only given unto ourselves, on wants, our selfish selves, one's love is not enough for another's but on theirs that's not honest, not one... not one immortal is given Satan's right

Satan

Death we eat, while we chew with demons
Demons around us as we let them in, our safe place, our home, our mind during a
world of perfection of a whirl wind of past memories and hurtful incidents, attacks
us each step of the way reminding us of threats n unhappiness, lies to be exact, of
what's not going to happen but worse if given time, given you, someone who doesn't
accepts you not care for your well or others being, shooting self-up with trust in
the wrong eyes of misconfusion of whom we worship too, the bad guy that is.. we
are bad because of fears or bad upon selfish of ones need... innocence of perfection
of every given talent was born, imperfections were created by lies n fears

Direction

What are we without natural pain, formed or given... natural pain with healing power born with passion to conquer the lesson... to excel the circumstances of life given equations, equations of wrong, wrong n could correct answers that's makes no sense of the plan given, teachers with reasons, answers to every solution but the solution to win, to learn n accept life that's given but not handed, head in the right direction if I make the right decision.. pain routes I make given human... life on Earth, given hearts I hurt upon apologies n sadness, apologizes for the mistaken one I knew you were, thought u were do too every one doing the same, sipping n feeling the pain, trying to find heal n a corrupted plan, do to given pain we hide the pain, we do more pain On things we don't see the same...

Together

No love surrounds me like yours do, no heart, no body, no physical attraction nor My mental Mind Can See another but attracts a You from me. You is mine but you is ours, a one we come for, for help, for guidance, for words we can't put together, but u bring us together, to share, to not hide but find ones an another the common fears we have over anxiety, to bring peace to another to fight the man n not be one with man, to become one but love to forgive but punish one's ability to be another not accept nor love thyself, self-cherish we can't give, only ones have self-taught, to love is loving another but self-love is first love, I'll help, I'll heal.. ones love can't compare to another love just combines forces to one whole spirit, a man and a woman, a man and man one's spirit is calling onto us to our mental attraction

Be Self

Words supposed to mean what is showed
Culture is difference due to the fact that we split up like animals around danger, race
is judgement do to one's ability to think n see different, one's character is different,
ones ability is different, one's shape is similar but ones heart is same until bruised,
nor fixed in surroundings of cruelty & chattered voices of unwilling friendships
of rules of life.. rules of life these are... not the same, not corrupted or corrected but
vanished on different Sides but the right side. Rules that involve Life to the extreme
before extreme meant dangerous, risky, but extreme in a spiritual bonding Turing
immortal, turning full of life in nature, to technology, but self-healing, self-love n
self-talent will... Chemicals surrounds the air like Satan which controls ours, study
ours, money built on trees but more of wealth and looks of smarts of mind living on
hate. Ones can't have done to their god but our god, our spirit will be more than
one man. Currency is just a number, but currency doesn't define who I am.

The One

I be walking in the light during the night, during dark clouds in dark vision, headed
towards the sight of short stops, of power play and strategy stops, of let's not hear but
listen in the hidden messages of secret talks, of secret love n secret spots. Of hidden
faces that's not able to talk, in forms of understanding and clear missions in a state
of forgiveness that ones have for abusive in verbal state, not physical but physically
emotionally in ones to know my emotional state to know my edges and n my curves
of beauty, to know ones plan to know how to be one to move on n to stand on in a
world of acceptance n approval.. one's true love is enough for many others, is enough
for families and animals for any living creature that beats on steps called mission

You're the one

Your all the things that's beautiful, your all of the things that I thought I couldn't have, your everything everyone always thought of but couldn't dream of, I can't believe your mine... you saved me from myself, you saved me from my enemies, you saved me when my mind was corrupted, from jealousy of others, n insecurities of my approach, I judged thee, n bullied thee but you saw right through me... u cleaned me up and polished me, u made me open up n see pass dimmed lights, shadows that surrounds me during the light, never thought I could love, never thought I could change, never thought I could see you shinning besides me. I was hungry and tired n u came n saved me Saving me from nightmares and smooth talkers, to night walkers n Hurtful things that comes upon us through life and lessons... that's gets me out of character but joy came n brung me light, held me tight and loved me right... that cheers for me when I'm losing or right that tells me when wrong but make it alright, that's there through darkness n pain..... u saved me from the opposite side of life that's more than love...

Front

Your craziness excites me in every way
U taunt and scar, I stare and look
There's more to you than you see...
Your tough guy imagine...
It's just a front, it's not you,
I see you, I see yourself, Your bad & your Good
You Can't get away from me
& I Can't hide from you
You Mine & I'm yours. Our Craziness for Love and
Strength will Move us Further than Light
No one can see but us, no one can bear us
That fire and darkness, that light that shines bright, through us we move during the
night... Our Tranquility, Our Love for another... Is Stronger, Is Wiser, We
Move Closer to be One, To Be Each Other in a Dark Place we Call VOICE

We Waiting

God's grace is given unto you with no mistakes no distractions, no rude people nor bad demons here to interrupt you during this amazing process of life n heavens, spiritual beings turned into sinners, to be born heavenly but cast here to view more, to view more n cherish more of his creations... distractions are near to destroy your mind n damage your gifts, fortune is turned into fake faith now false prophets, for steak n lobster in the destruction of the opposite of good, the opposite of real but fake, I can't take n won't take of what's mine, I won't destroy my fate but I will fight for my fate, I won't seek him but I will destroy him through many obstacles I Make, he make. He guilds me through the earth n what's good n what's here for my destiny to take place... I'll grow and bloom while speak with prosper n no despair... I'll help n plant the seeds that were unnoticed to fly in be a part of him that's now known... for our blessings is waiting in the unknown

The Holy Bible is our everyday lives

-Erica Rayvon

The bible is more than a Scripture or words, it's the world around us, it's the path of life, that plans the world and the form given to us. We're all created and assigned to give, to love, to conquer all evil approached to us. Jesus is the creator of all things, Satan is the destruction of a start to finish, once started it's hard to get out, but a strong voice of such can Heal and Save numerous lives that's god given us, a freedom of Life and a tongue to give life unto others, the word of happiness and joy, the insides that makes us tingle, the inside it's a spirit of Hope and Honesty, the right path the right rode to righteous. Religious is a part of our everyday lives around us. Don't destroy thee or others for a deal you don't know what's hidden beneath.

Unreal

Real is power no matter how unreal or how unsafe u think it is but is, it's really appreciated and really admired really admired by beauties and talented lost souls that's taken for granted in Satan's creation. The false that is unreal but real, the brainwash that money rule everything but truth is the answer. that voice is the gift of all creations and wisdom is the key to earth, that no man shall love you more than others but preaches, truth is living life on earth shall not live In hell, shall not kill the known but prophet the ones who know… to succeed in a world of brainwash n materialist of media of sales and phony's but of life and acknowledge to conquer the life and evil that surrounds us, to beat liquor n drugs that man given us to fill high but High on butterflies and beautifully things…to love natural beauty n to love an artist to listen in follow the artist, to try to give hope n acknowledge, but gone like fast food orders, fast cars in fast food n chemical stances… Poison around us.. thy shall not pick the fruit but swim the lake

Admire You

Admire our beauty through shapes and settings
Voices of others that admire differences and, our body and soul make up one to be One
within Our Spirit through One's Mind and Expressions, our intellect can be tricky
but One Guts, one's Spirit, one's whole being can be aware or admiration, our talents
and gifts are aspired but not admire to be admire to one's self worth, self-soul and self-
righteous to not be approved or want others approval to not like themselves for one's
approval, self-admiration is Self-love is One's self being to be you in Your beautiful
flaws and habits, understanding others is Self-wisdom, is Acknowledge to know others
in good trait to good being of admiration to accept self-admiration is To Accept others

Follows of mine power to your ability of strength of mind is controlled over a figure of objective of a blind behind a glass of harden walls of trees block night of your sense of power to another's, more on your hides over the fence of life above the saint of sins, less power of saints lays in the fakest of truth that discovers church of spirits beings preached on magic of implanted rules that think fake light is bright and wrong is right but shapes are idols to hold on to cages of crosses of X shaped wronged of creative minds see out the X

Blood

Family is what holds us together...
through laughter to teary tears to abominable joy that cripples our hearts out
to make full of Hurt and pain to Light and Life. A life that's filled
up with unhappiness and Disguises... Our family is the only thing we
have that's blood, our genes n DNA combines Our wide noises to
big foreheads, to identical to fraternal we hurt all the same way
We Eat all day, we toast to cheer to volunteer to be near on another
spreading cheer... Spreading Hope and highs...
N separating our Lows & Lies

Imagination

Our imagination is a story told in our mind, of fun and solutions, a thought of imagination that bright up lights and signals in world of letters n poems, a universe of spirits that combines one energy into one's whole, a whole of goodness and sweet joy, a whole that won't come Close to a evil spirit that gets us out of you, gets us out of our spirit n goodwill, our fortune n transition came near to a bad one or bad things. A spirit that makes sparks fly into electro lights, our energy combines into one's half to one's unit, to one's gram, to one's ounce to pound, of tears reaching on to one's hand to be ONE w/your Kindness to be not a Couple, but an empire, A relieving feeling

"Jesus Lives Within"

A piece of God Lives within,
That connects a spiritual intellectual feeling of wisdom and power,
A power of wealth and Love, a Piece of Joy that
Only Heals the broken in a disguise;
but seek thee in the spirit of Whole
To grow and plant seeds to strengthen minds and shape beings,
to lead a direction of righteous in Will to his Good Will, to his
Words and actions to his stories in reflection that
I am half of thee a peace of mind that channels Energy that's deeper
than WE, A earth that counts on me! On WE! Shall we
Prosper in a deed of Whole n Humbleness or Deceit and dumbness,
shall we fail, or shall we proceed but to succeed in his need...

Age

Out the womb I was, between the towels I am
Fresh and ready, from a start to a finish, through a cord and between a line,
where life comes crashing in and splashes You three different times
A Kid, too Teen, Adult.
same body, same person...
Different places turn into different dreams, to new experiences, to new Adventures,
two words to one story, a decision based on a lifetime. A lifetime with no regrets, a
Lifetime worth waiting, carefree... Lifeless. A dream come true, with fairytales
and laughter a dream worth waiting. Beyond the lust and Lies a new Love
awaits in your times... A new life for you, wise choices, wise life, a wise one will
carry on, for wisdom for you, for us to carry on... Through generations to lean

I'm Here

Love yourself more than life, more than others, more than things n fast
life, more than any living thing that takes you away from you...
Shelters you in a black hole without life, without air... just doubt and Disturbance
Disturbance to the absolute wrath till you scream NO! no more...
No more walls... No more ceilings, just air and ME...
Completely ME...
No Sidelines, Bystanders, no problems, no stress
just you and your worth...
Completely silent, completely focus Different shades of Arouse meant... Gets me excited
in the deepest areas around my articles, around my lungs! I Sing, I Shout, I
Whisper without a shame or doubt I'm here, I'm free to show you who I am n what
I do... I'm here... To be all I can be... I'm HERE Without guilt, without You!

*"To change another is
to change thyself"*

-Erica Rayvon

*Every day I wanna cry
Every day I wanna Die, I wanna not be me nor do the things you say,
I wanna live n be carefree, I wanna live n be me, independence is key... I
don't wanna be here, I don't want less, nor help, I hate big headed man, I
hate power, I hate judgmental people, ion like you nor love you, ion know
why I Try, ion know I choose to be here, ion know why I'm still here*

Inside Looking Out

I don't understand why I was made to fit in a world of such difference in judgement...
Of hate and Lust with Cruel intentions w/ Bad character and lack of
life, lack of Value and lack of Care... Not understanding or looking
outside but inside, stuck in the middle... Of Jury and Judges... Of
Law in Order... Of not peace nor fair but Envy and Lies...
Understand why I'm this or that... I Seek equally, I See different, I see Lost souls
and confused minds... I see a person who don't belong, I see a mind that stand alone...

Sorry

I wake up in a empty bed every morning
Wishing u would awake
Appear in the blue in the sky
Between the sheets in my bed
Between my legs, caressing my thighs
Caressing my breasts n shielding my heart
Protecting it from the earth, from mankind
To be one, to understand me, you
To understand the emptiness this world has
To understand the emptiness my bed has w/o
There's no comparison of what I feel for you
There's no love I'll never trade for you
You the Rock of solids outsides of air through gas that vanishes
but rock stands, on my grass, covers, to teach me, to honor the
strength over air, to share the happiness u give when near

I Won't you

It's that time again
That time of the month
When I crave for u
While I wait for you
Your arrival
Your past stories
And soft touches
Your back rubs n crafted pastries
your voice n presence
Is not enough, I want your soul
To tend to me in my every need
My every desire that I prosper
Your natural being of self-soul
I'm your last
Ur last breath ur last step on earth
Cherish me in my being
My soul being my mind being my whole
Like I'm your whole... apart of you
I'm your need for survival, your last quest of joy and
happiness to meet your beginning and ending
Treat me like I'm your last

Anniversary

Today was the day...
Today was the day you friended me
To know my thoughts, my glory, my worth
To seek my acknowledgement and wisdom
To become more than a relationship but a marriage
A union to be one, to be accepted n taken, to be open and honest
To share the light of earth, the heaven we cherish n perish, the beauty of it all
We inhale it, we live it, we own it
We are our own voice, our own leader, our own person, to be known in the approval
of secrets and loyalty. To feel each other emotional, physically and sexual.
Our love loyalty and trust, we pact to promise, to forever to the
omega come, we are the beginning, were not the end
Never leave, never dishonest, never betray
We stay solid through all the trails of life
We are each other ♥

Anyday Now

Any day I will be in your arms towards your chest on the side of your rest
I will feel your warmth
I will feel your love, like nothing before
A bond that forever gets better
As the day's flies by, as the streetlights dim right
I'll be your star shinning bright
In the sky up high
On the stage you love
In my possession you crave...
I love you more everyday
Threw the fights in the bliss
I'll never fade away
Just a few more days I'll be with you forever
Through thick n thin I'll never betray
I'll never disobey, along as you stay
I'll never go, on top like soil beneath
The testicles of soft balls u weak on time... on top, wanting more
Craving more, in you so deep you want more
You feel my heart in mind, you seek more
But can u handle more
Just a few more days before we intertwine 🌢

Action

I see flicks
After flicks
Wishing upon a dick
A princess for a prince
Dreaming of a dream
upon reality
I look for excitement
I find your existence
I wonder how u feel
I wonder how u feel in me
A touch so wanting
A kiss so gentle
A love so great
Only one can satisfy
Only one can come by
After me, after you
I found myself lusting you
Craving you
Wanting u to feel how I feel
Wanting your desires to be mine
Wanting you to Be min

Were Meant

Are we meant to be together at this time of age, generation where love is just a word and care is just a joke, the jokes we make to keep us, the trails we go threw to keep strong, you tell me right, u tell me wrong, u tell me things u not sure, I tell you what's sure of, sure of life, sure of you, me, sure of many things that come towards us, they don't belong to try to divide us, I'm sure of my love for you is here, I'm sure each movements we make is ours, a plan for our future, a plan that will last, a plan for our marriage is sure to come

Your Perfection

You can't be mad for allowing yourself to befriend another... on
the consequences and the withdrawal within that decision
Can only be mad at thyself for opening up and trusting that someone, being there
and helping that someone, Caring for and accepting that Someone... U can only
be Mad at yourself for being the best of yourself, the best YOU, your Nature
and Goodwill will Follow through.. U must know n learn before u give and love
You must have the strength to get up n learn from your mistakes to carry on
You must accept people actions and willingness to learn from their sins... There
troubles n misconduct will not be approved nor Taken for granted but lead n
helped... You must know who to love n trust... What u do n who u hurting,
Drains Energy from our spirits within... giving chances n holding faith...?
to accept the choices, you make to conquer the enemy... To
pass the enemy, to learn him n Know thyself... To not lose
YOURSELF but to better Yourself in your careless acts.

"Dreams are Just Goals"

-Erica Rayvon

Today is a new Day
To better yourself, educate family n friends, give wisdom and acknowledgement
to companies and fortune about your good worth, theirs's
Your good Being and Accomplishments
To brag, to feel good, about you and life, not worrying about tomorrow or next
week problems, to be blessed n grateful that you in this! Apart of this....
Apart of this System that Makes us Strive and Work... To Work or Show
Worth, To Drain to be Better than What we Never thought we'll be... To Get
up off ours to live, to inspire. To raise above... To make it from Business Casual
to Formal. To glide into work wearing what wants because you made it...
Today is the Day I think about my Career
I think about the bigger picture, making it through the
Week. Making it a Lifestyle for a lifetime
Today is the Day I think about my dreams

I Don't fit

I don't fit and a society of Followers & Manipulators
liars and cheaters
Actions to change, I Don't fit... I can't squeeze the lemon when
there's no juice, I Can't pick an apple when there's no life
I Can't Change who I am to be whole
I can't be More than birth
Rules help those who Obey, those who Learn, those who listen
Teach me, teach you,
Stand up for those who need voice
For those who Who's Weak & washed
In a world that changes them through ads n media, fakeness through heart to soul,
To be considered beautiful n someone else vision but yours... Not comfortable in your
own shell but comfortable n someone else vision? What's love? What's Society?
I don't fit...

Stubborn

I need you everyday
I want you everyday
But I don't need you everyday
I need to find myself n love myself
Know myself n cherish myself
Go back to my family & find myself
Find my Star in the Galaxy, A vietary of traits, learn more for me to know you
For us to be A WE, alone is Independent, Dependent is Team Spirit! I
Want you to be there, i need you to Know, Me & why i do n say the things i
do, Why my spirit So Polar n my Heart So Pure, i Must Learn to accept
n forgive, to forgive is to forget, all these Quests & Journeys is a Must, it's
something i Don't understand, We Don't! That's higher than us. A Hole I
been Pushed for my Stubbornness & Tounge, On Bads of good. i Need you n
I Want you. it's a thing I must Admit. don't push me back for stubbornness

I adore you

You make my skin crawl
My skin curver
My hairs perking
My heart beats
My world stops i love…
Your voice makes me cry
The sound of you moves me
Touch me
Saddens me that you're not here
With me i love
To you

Threw me

Your spirit awakens me
No one can compare what u do to me
I love you too
Like Simba to wild
Like Jesus to angels
A love for you
Every second im not by
I break, i cry. I try to be strong, what would i do.. in a world so cold like the ice, so cold like Everest so big like Texas. Put yourself in my shoes n love like i love, like blood like love my own that's within me... Made me, love me, taught me, teach me, i need you to grow i need u to help me see all i can see in a world so cold n lonely n a world so wrong so heartless, love me like a wife like im your all like self like mother teaching u right from wrong, like a childhood friends who knows yours sins...i love you so.. I love u more than u think... I love u more than you'll ever know

Headwraps & Hairstyles

What's a color without a headwrap to match my fly in hair in or out the wrap,
rap or wrap the type of hair to match my rap when I wrap my head in a
wrap, my hair is busy in the knots I call stress but the best the wrap the less
the test of stress, free of knots and tangles of my wrap of free and wild wild and
free my hair will be me an idea to match my style no matter color or style show
beauty of long or short without hair without wrap my face makes hair

Dance

Music to my ears from the winds and voice playing in war is the voice of love and talent, the steps of rock to rap to the steps of feet dancing in the sunlight no heat no sweat the beauty of light is the beauty of the wood of the wild, Africa's beauty of trees and green grass that blossoms the roots to the beauties of the pedals, the lyrics to the song is the spirit to my soul, free and lite jumps of joy swinging hands and lifting heads, I'm happy when I see the beauty of others lyrics

Birthday

It's My Day to make a difference, my birthday is my birth right to breath air and see the light in person from heaven once known succeeded and made works of others of gods beauty unto them! My birthday will bring light to myself and other every soul will feel mine spirit onto my day to be everyone's day to celebrate with me, a day we met brung laughs to keep you mine to keep you in my prayers in my days here on this planet of earth, Celebrate the days we here another year of three hundred and sixty five days of my minutes of growing, processing and comprehending my message to give my plan of why I'm here thank you for celebrating with me

Shell

It started with a smile, a young smile with a heart full of gold, never wondered or saw one so full, not of self but life on silver won't turn gold that can't change, a kiss of argument of your touches of sweet words, I can't share, wouldn't share of my selfish needs I have for you, my love I wouldn't turn a caterpillar to a butterfly your beauty is the wings of colors you have made me saw from beast to beauty, beauty I hid beneath my shell

What is Health?

What is Sickness? How it starts why it start? Wind blows with pure air? Fresh air so why I'm sick? Germs on others but how they get there? Wind blows but my spirit cold? Why here in the world of many disease... sickness of no help only when needed to your help to help, what is Sickness? Given to im fine, wake up, im fine, can't breath im fine. Breaths on snores through mouth, can't breath through my nose, on snot threw air when born on air, silent, no aware, are natural, on snores unhealthy on to my age, sickness of addictive substances added to make me sick in other parts, substances that's there but added to on the world I call ours, ours, sickness what is health?

Sweet and Sour

Noodles free and slippery, slimmy and soy sweet with sour, taste in noodles, taste in sauce, sour not in my taste of sweet, soft, natural, right, sending love from a mixture taste, two different flavors of 2 different feels, spreading sweetness to your sweet behavior of sweet, cabin chills with wooden stools, paper plates of sweet delights, the same delights we pursue the warm weather of delight

Humanity

So many like you I can't stand to put up with you, waste breath and waste tears, you are the reflection of you, your choices, your mistakes you bring yourself happiness on your choices, decisions you call you can't make no calls, no freedom, let your power come up, let your soul speak, sad I can't speak, sad I can't help, you one with him, you one with anger, madness you bring on self n others, why pain those who appreciate? Why push out love? Some lost, confused it's not my mistake... spoke on life, spoke on real, how you feel, are you life or are you death? I give you humanity

Nothing lasts forever

Nothing Last forever but a heart and a spirit, a spirit that's brave enough to keep the world calm, and Company, green and great.. bad times never last like whipped cream on a pumpkin pie, living on yo mine not a stress to live your best must sin on broken things that wouldn't keep, healthy or right, we right built on love and patience, patience took time but thought easily, love created beauty, hate created death, nothing lasts forever on my selfish behavior, disappears, lifeless no meaning on this circle of air, keeping still but shouting life, I must live like forever, i must live like death has no life, no start no beginning, my life of age 0, free and many years of life

Man-made Technology will always fail us

-Erica Rayvon

Outdoors is taken from my mind my fun my life, taken control of mine my ones who see, enjoy we, taken from ours, our hands, brains we can't learn or see the tech control we, must have must hold why my mind is not in control who is he who is why my addiction taken control of thee why u see me through a phone on my protected one, on lies of behaviors u took to keep me use me an my way of human, I'm human not tech, im spiritual not human, not to be used in thrown away not burnt, I'm human not technology, I'm one of life not death

Approach

I am my outside appearance I am me no matter how formed or taught come to me as a way of respect how I am given to you, how I see you, seeing actions on movement respect is growth, respect is build and grow with another, not just mine but onto others approach is my definition of character how u speak onto others, must not care how others see you, but on how u see yourself how less of others u are, must not see me but see others, to judge is to be judged why not fool you or fool yourself u are the fool for seeing you

Abuse

Verbal abuse you give me, physical abuse u uses me

I can't like you nor love you

You irritating, what a bully

when High you make me Low,

when n confidence u make me wonder, u make me feel less, u make me feel unwanted,

disrespect, u shelter, u make me feel unwanted, u make me regret loving you, wishing

u was here, wishing i were home. U make me not wanted for Love nor care but

death and hatred, feelings of pain n riots, fire and shadows, blood and scars

Your deceitful..

I showed u life, I showed u love.. I showed not everything is

not what it seemed but misunderstood n other ways of thoughts.. I

showed u positive when negative, rich when poor, hurt to fix

n happiness when all hope Is gone..

I can't continue to feel ashamed when known, to feel guilty of

other insecurities but inspired n cared for the ungrateful..

Unappreciated I am

Believe

I'm gone leave one of these days, when the sun sets and the day ends,
when the birds rest and the cats lay
Alone and peaceful when my smile shines, no negativity, no voices, just nature
and my covers, travelling far from deceit and demons, users and drainers, wash
away happiness and joy.. Fleas and ticks nagging as your blood warms ice, Runs
cold with your soul, pushes away kittens and puppies with wicked souls and metal
hearts, good intentions w/ good Directions, u lead me down to success along with
stress and poisoned minds, poison walks with poison thoughts, poison things along
with poison people.. Drains me, angers me! shows me who I am or who I'm not!
U push me to danger n Disease, Lies and Hurt you give to me! U beat me with
past n try to insult me with lust, lust n lean Im not, strong and brave I am
I shall not condemn n evil doings that shall benefit me but train those to
love the n help them like my own.. A team to build a mind to conquer

Unconditionally

Love me when I'm sick n old, not cute n fit
Love me unconditionally, not inconsistency
I'm here for you through the rain n downpour
Through site seeing n rainbows,
love me unconditionally
Love brings people together through sports n hobbies, fashion to sexualities,
icons to god's, it's the things we love that makes us human
People, places n things were all one body just tryna be perfect, trying
to connect, tryna be here, look like this, dress like that,
love me unconditionally,
unconditionally love...
through my addictions, my wealth, my health, my mind my heart,
my soul my dreams I need unconditionally support, unconditionally
truth n honesty. I need unconditionally love from you to be me

Selfish

Don't lie to me to make me feel better
Don't feel sorry for me for not getting it right
Im stuck in my ways n you stuck n yours
Can we be mad?
Can we be mad for not understanding each other life n not wanting to learn?
Yes? Maybe so ? Selfish is not love, Selfish is not pure
Im Stuck in this body with my pride held high
Im High in this life of power but chains holds me against others
Im stuck with rules n regulations not fitting in or playing
the part, im Amazed at how im living
Im here, open, scheduled, timed... Im here...
Im stuck in circles n merry go rounds cause of my Trust Issues...
I'm chained n towered with love & hate by Ones i Can't name...
Im stuck n my ways.. My pride is my sin & My Eagerness. is my downfall

Valentines Day

Valentine's day is near
Valentines day is hear
But u not here
Your loves forbidden
A treasure in the seas beneath
A Rare love thats rare to find
A love that we all want
To be accepted, to be kind and sweet
abnormal to most but perfect to few
A love thats forever and Immortal
A love thats takes year's to find
A forbidden love i say
Only in fairytales, myths and fiction
Only in Forbidden islands with
Animals thats not here to see
A love i need to feel safe and secure
A love u need to keep guarded and warm
A passion like fireworks and shooting stars
That get our heart jumping like jumping jacks
A safe love a healthy love that will keep us living everlasting...

I Won't

You hate me
You love me
U difficult
U confusing
U can't! I Won't!
U make me Right
U make u me fight
U make so mad that i dislike you
Like...
I can't... You... You just...
I can't.. (Sign) you just to good
To bad for me, to powerful for me
Not right for me.. I cnt with u
I won't with u.. U just.. So damn fine):
U give me headaches n stomach aches
U make my skin crawl... mannn (giggles)
I can't with u ☹

Vowels

I love you
I hate you
I trust you
My wellbeing its yours
Mines is ours
Ours is yours
Love you to pieces
To Mars to Earth
To Earth to Mars
I Set Sail
Beneath your trails
Below we go
Arise we shine
From hell to heaven
To Heaven to hell
We Fight like Rope
We high ass dope
On many adventures we strive
Like Martin an Gina
We laugh we joke
Together for always
Our vowels be kept

CPSIA information can be obtained
at www.ICGtesting.com
Printed in the USA
BVHW031132050919

557660BV00007B/170/P